P

Imagine Me on a Sit-Ski!

George Moran

Illustrated by Nadine Bernard Westcott

Albert Whitman & Company, Morton Grove, Illinois

To my father, Frank Moran. G.M.

*To the Vermont Handicapped
Ski and Sports Association. N.B.W.*

Library of Congress Cataloging-in-Publication Data

Moran, George, 1948-
Imagine me on a sit-ski! / George Moran;
illustrated by Nadine Bernard Westcott.
p.   cm.
Summary: A child who has cerebral palsy and uses a wheelchair
describes learning to ski with adaptive equipment.
ISBN 0-8075-3618-0
[1. Skis and skiing—Fiction. 2. Cerebral palsy—Fiction.
3. Physically handicapped—Fiction.]
I. Westcott, Nadine Bernard, ill. II. Title.
PZ7.M788195Im   1995   94-10806
[E]–dc20   CIP
                                                            AC

Text copyright © 1995 by George Moran.
Illustrations copyright © 1995 by Nadine Bernard Westcott.
Published in 1995 by Albert Whitman & Company,
6340 Oakton Street, Morton Grove, Illinois 60053.
Published simultaneously in Canada by
General Publishing, Limited, Toronto.
Printed in the United States of America.
10 9 8 7 6 5 4 3 2 1

The typeface is Stone Informal.
The illustrations are in watercolor and ink.
Design by Karen A. Yops.

Learning to ski meant a lot to me. I know that millions of people go skiing, but I never thought I could.

My name is Billy. I have to use a wheelchair all the time because I have cerebral palsy and I can't use my legs. I can use my arms a little, though.

Even though I understand everything you say to me, I can't talk to you with my voice. Instead, I talk by using my wordboard. I just point my finger at what I want to say. If the words I need aren't on my wordboard, I can spell them for you.

When Ms. Harris and Mr. Johnson told my class at school that they were going to take us skiing, I was really excited. But at the same time, I pointed out, I was **AFRAID**!

Ms. Harris told me that everyone is a little nervous about skiing for the first time. And Mr. Johnson said we would have instructors who were experts in helping people who are physically challenged learn to ski. I still felt a little scared, but I decided to try it.

We all grew more and more excited as we counted down the days. Finally it was time to go! I got into the van with seven of my school friends, and off we went.

It was a long ride up to Snow Valley. I was glad to have my best friend, Sara, sitting next to me. We told jokes and laughed the whole way. We were still laughing when the van pulled up in front of Snowshoe Lodge.

Whenever I go someplace new, I worry if it will be wheelchair accessible, which means that people can get in and out of places in their wheelchairs and that there aren't too many stairs. Ms. Harris had told me that the lodge was accessible, and she was right. It had a ramp at the entrance, and wide doors and hallways. There were a few problems, though, such as narrow bathrooms.

Mr. Johnson, Tommy, Devin, Kirby, and I moved our bags into our room, while Ms. Harris, Sara, Nicole, Kelly, and Marita moved into theirs.

After unpacking, we all got back in the van and went straight to the mountain to get our ski equipment ready for the next day.

When I saw the ski mountain, I was **SCARED**!

It looked so high and steep!

When we went inside the Snow Valley Handicapped Skiing Building, I felt a little better. There were lots of other people who were physically challenged getting ready to ski. Some of them said they had never skied before, just like me. Others said they had skied a lot, and they didn't seem scared at all.

The lodge had a lot of different kinds of equipment because there are many different types of disabilities. The instructors helped each of us find the right kind of adaptive equipment. Sara used a walker, so they gave her a special walker with little skis on the bottom, along with regular skis. Kirby and Nicole got crutches with tiny skis on them. Tommy and I each got a "sit-ski," which looks a little like a kayak.

After we had all finished getting our equipment, we went out to a nice restaurant for supper. Ms. Harris cut up my food for me. I can't use a knife and fork, so I have to pick up my food with my hands. It tastes just as good that way, though! It was really fun eating in a restaurant with all my friends.

We went back to the lodge together, where we talked and watched TV in the lounge. After a while, Mr. Johnson said we better get to bed because we had a busy day ahead of us. I was so excited I thought I'd be awake all night, but I was asleep as soon as my head hit the pillow.

When morning came, Ms. Harris and Mr. Johnson got us up early. They helped us shower and get dressed and took us out for breakfast. Then we headed back to the mountain.

This was it! My heart was racing!

My ski instructors, Jack and Cindi, were really nice. They seemed just as excited as I was. They helped me get into my sit-ski. Next they put some foam padding around me so I wouldn't slide around inside. Then they zipped me in so only my head and arms were showing. It was cold outside, but I was nice and warm in my sit-ski! Cindi hung my small wordboard, the one I use when I'm not in my wheelchair, around my neck. And Jack put a helmet on my head.

They explained to me how to turn the sit-ski by leaning to the side and pushing into the snow with one of the small ski poles they had given me. Pushing my right pole would make me go right, and pushing my left pole would make me go left. It sounded really easy.

I told them I was **READY**!

They hooked my sit-ski onto a snowmobile, tucked my wordboard inside my jacket, and off we went up the mountain!

What a fun ride! The snowmobile went so fast! About halfway up the mountain, we stopped in a wide, flat area that Jack said was a good place to practice. Then he took the snowmobile back down to get Tommy and his two instructors.

Cindi and Jack went over the instructions again. Jack attached the tether line to my sit-ski. He told me to raise my poles a little if I wanted to stop, and he would pull back on the tether. Then they pointed me downhill and gave me a push.

At first I went slow, but then I was going faster and faster! It was so exciting! I started getting scared again. I raised my arms, and Jack stopped me right away.

Cindi told me I should turn more to control my speed. Then we started down again. Cindi skied backwards and helped me turn by pushing the front of the sit-ski to one side, then the other. I worked harder on leaning to the side and using my poles. It really did help keep me from going too fast.

When we reached the bottom of the hill, we got on the snowmobile and went right back up again. Then we made another run. This time I felt better and didn't need as much help. After some more runs I was really getting the hang of it. I was having so much fun I almost hated to stop for lunch. Almost, but not quite. Skiing had really made me **HUNGRY**!

I met my friends back in the lodge. We were all so excited telling each other about our morning's adventures that Ms. Harris had to keep reminding us to eat. Sara laughed when she told me how many times she had fallen. "I just got right back up again and kept on going," she said. Sara's like that; she never gives up. Tommy told me he really liked his sit-ski. Everybody was doing really well and having a great time.

After lunch we had many more runs. I kept doing better and better, having more fun each time. One time I guess I became overly confident. I let myself get going too fast and wiped out when I tried to turn. It was a little scary, but it didn't hurt a bit, thanks to my helmet and padding. Cindi laughed and said, "Well, now you know you can wipe out and not get hurt!"

When it was time to quit for the day, Jack told me that I was ready to go on the chairlift up to a higher part of the mountain. I really felt **PROUD**!

We went to that nice restaurant again for supper. Afterwards we returned to the lodge and stayed up for a little while, swapping stories about our experiences on the slopes. We went to bed pretty soon, though, because we were all really **TIRED**!

Back at the mountain the next morning, Cindi and Jack kept their promise. They helped me into my sit-ski and took me over to the chairlift. When it was our turn to get on, the operator stopped it for us. Cindi and Jack lifted me in my sit-ski right up onto the chair. Then they sat on either side of me, and off we went up the mountain. What a thrill! I felt like a real, honest-to-goodness skier. Imagine—me riding on a chairlift.

The ride to the top was fantastic! I was so high off the ground. I was even looking down at the treetops.

We got off at the top with all the other skiers. What a view we had! We could see miles away across the mountains. Jack and Cindi let me enjoy the view for a while. Then they pulled my sit-ski ahead to the "fall-line." That's where the ground starts to go downwards, and you start to slide.

"Remember," said Cindi, "use your poles to help you turn, and lift your arms if you want to stop."

"Are you ready?" asked Jack.

I nodded my head.

They gave my sit-ski a little push, and I started sliding downhill. I felt a little scared again because this slope was steeper and longer. I knew how to turn now, though. And I knew I could trust Jack and Cindi to stop me. So I wasn't too scared.

It was a much longer run than the one I had skied the day before. I had to make a lot of turns, and I stopped twice. But I made it all the way to the bottom without wiping out.

We took the chairlift back up again and again.
One time we ran into Tommy and his instructors. Tommy
challenged me to a race to the bottom. I won!

Each time down the mountain I let myself go faster and faster. I had never moved so fast in my life! It was pure joy just sliding down the mountain! I felt so free! I never wanted it to end.

That evening, back at the lodge, we all talked and talked about what a great time we had had skiing. We asked Ms. Harris and Mr. Johnson if we could stay just one more day. They laughed and said they would love to, but we had to get back to school.

"**SCHOOL? WHAT'S THAT?**" I spelled.

We all laughed.

Well, my ski trip is over, and I'm back home. It's great to remember all the things I did there and all the fun I had with my friends. I know that I'll go skiing again sometime. I just hope it's soon.

Now I wonder what other sports I might be able to try. I bet scuba diving would be great! I'd love to swim among all those colorful fish and coral, the way they do on those nature shows on TV.

Come to think of it, Ms. Harris did tell us about a group called "Wheels 'n Waves" that teaches scuba diving to people who are physically challenged. Hmmmmm. . .